"Critics' Pick!"   —*Time Out New York*

"Judith Thompson paints a richly textured portrait....
Thompson defiantly scrapes to the marrow of opposing
camps, offering a lament that is theological and tragic
and contains a rare, eerie beauty."

—*LA Weekly*

"Perspectives on Iraq vividly staged."

—*Studio City Sun*

"*Palace of the End* thrills as much as it disturbs, leaving
the viewer, if not a better, surely a wiser person."

—*Bloomberg*

"*Palace of the End*... never crosses the line of abject mor-
alizing. The issues are presented as theatre; the voice is
focused, commanding. The truth is a catharsis for
redemption."

—*Tolucan Times*

"Beautifully poetic and brutally graphic."

—*The NY Daily News*

"As the curtain call ended, a stranger said to me 'That
was *intense*. I mean, God. Wow!' "

—NYTheatre.com

"*Palace of the End* raises the bar. ...beautifully specific
writing... packs a mean punch... as quietly unforgettable
as it is purposely rending."

—*LA Times* Critics Choice

PALACE OF THE END

Also by Judith Thompson

Body & Soul
Capture Me
The Crackwalker
Enoch Arden in the Hope of Shelter
Habitat
Lion in the Streets
Palace of the End
Perfect Pie
Sled
Such Creatures
White Biting Dog

PALACE OF THE END

JUDITH THOMPSON

PLAYWRIGHTS CANADA PRESS
TORONTO

PLAYWRIGHTS CANADA PRESS
The Canadian Drama Publisher
215 Spadina Ave., Suite 230, Toronto, ON Canada M5T 2C7
phone 416.703.0013   fax 416.408.3402
orders@playwrightscanada.com • www.playwrightscanada.com

For professional or amateur production rights, please contact
Great North Artists Management
350 Dupont St., Toronto, ON M5R 1V9
phone 416.925.2051

Playwrights Canada Press acknowledges the financial support of the Government of Canada through the Canada Book Fund and the Canada Council for the Arts and the Province of Ontario through the Ontario Arts Council and the Ontario Media Development Corporation for our publishing activities.

Cover artwork by Nuska Prijatelj
Production editor / Cover design by JLArt

LIBRARY AND ARCHIVES CANADA CATALOGUING IN PUBLICATION

Thompson, Judith, 1954-
Palace of the end / Judith Thompson--Rev. 2nd ed.

A play.
ISBN 978-0-88754-835-2

1. Iraq War, 2003- --Drama. I. Title
PS8589.H4883P34 2008   C812'.54   C2008-904095-3

First edition: November 2007
Second edition: July 2008
Fourth printing: December 2010

Printed and bound in Canada by Gauvin Press, Gatineau

The author encourages readers of this play to donate to the following charity, which has been endorsed by Dr. Thabit A.J. Abdullah:

Iraqi Alamal Association
Karadah, Al-Alwiah, Sector 903, Road 14, Number 6
(Road opposite Alwiyah Telecommunication Office)
Alwia, Baghdad, Iraq

Website: www.iraqi-alamal.org

The author's royalties from the sale of this book are going to this charity.

Dedicated to:

Connie Rooke
a visionary, brilliant editor, great beauty
and inspiration to women everywhere

&

the thousands of Iraqi children who have endured
unimaginable suffering for so very long

Playwright's Note

Each of these three monologues is based on news stories or research on events involving the real person named as the speaker, but the persona or character of each speaker has been created by me, and everything other than the real events springs from my imagination.

My Pyramids was inspired by the media circus around Lynndie England, the American soldier convicted of the sexual torture of Iraqi detainees in Abu Ghraib prison.

Harrowdown Hill was inspired by the well publicized events surrounding the public life and solitary death of Dr. David Kelly, the British weapons inspector and microbiologist.

Instruments of Yearning was inspired by the true story of Nehrjas Al Saffarh, a well-known member of the Communist party of Iraq, who was tortured by Saddam Hussein's secret police in the 1970s. She died when her home was bombed by the Americans in the first Gulf War.

Acknowledgements

Palace of the End is based on the monologue play *My Pyramids* by Judith Thompson, first read at the Toronto political cabaret, The Wrecking Ball in 2004. The premiere production was subsequently produced by Volcano at the Traverse Theatre in Edinburgh, August 2005. Director: Ross Manson, Lynndie England: Waneta Storms, Lighting Designer: Rebecca Picherack, Stage Manager: JP Robichaud.

Palace of the End was commissioned by Epic Theatre Ensemble and received a developmental workshop with the company in June, 2006.

Teatro Limonaia in Florence, Italy, produced a staged reading of both *My Pyramids* and *Instruments of Yearning* in October, 2006.

Further developed with the Canadian Stage Company, Toronto, 2007.

Special thanks to Rena Zimmerman for dramaturgy help with *Harrowdown Hill* and to Ann Anglin and Julian Richings who participated in the stage readings of the play for ARCfest Toronto, in October 2006.

Palace of the End was first produced by 49th Parallel Theatre in association with Open At The Top at The NOHO Arts Center, North Hollywood, California, in June 2007 with the following company:

KATE MINES   Soldier
MICHAEL CATLIN   Dr. David Kelly
ANNA KHAJA   Nehrjas Al Saffarh

Directed by Sara Botsford and CB Brown
Lighting Design   Luke Moyer
Sound Design   Alfred Madain
Stage Manager   Mark Heath

• • •

Palace of the End received its Canadian Premiere by the Canadian Stage Company at the Berkeley Theatre, Toronto in January 2008 with the following company:

MAEV BEATY   Soldier
JULIAN RICHINGS   Dr. David Kelly
ARSINEE KHANJIAN   Nehrjas Al Saffrah

Directed by David Storch
Set and Costume Design   Teresa Przybylski
Lighting Design   Kimberly Purtell
Composer/Sound Design   John Gzowski
Stage Manager   Marinda De Beer

• • •

Palace of the End received its New York Premiere by Epic Theatre Ensemble (Zak Berkman, Founding Director of Artistic Programming) at the Peter Jay Sharp Theatre, June 23, 2008 with the following company:

TERI LAMM   Soldier
ROCCO SISTO   Dr. David Kelly
HEATHER RAFFO   Nehrjas Al Saffrah

Directed by Daniella Topol
Set Design   Mimi Lien
Lighting Design   Justin Townsend
Costume Design   Theresa Squire
Sound Design   Ron Russell
Projection Design   Leah Gelpe
Original Music   Katie Down
Stage Manager   Brenna St. George Jones

PALACE OF THE END

MY PYRAMIDS
HARROWDOWN HILL
INSTRUMENTS OF YEARNING

Characters

SOLDIER, female
DR. DAVID KELLY
NEHRJAS AL SAFFARH

My Pyramids

Music over:

A SOLDIER, Dr. DAVID Kelly, and NEHRJAS Al Saffarh all enter, as if through a looking glass, and take their places.

The SOLDIER, nine months pregnant, speaks facing the audience, to an imaginary Quebec landlady:

SOLDIER   *Bonjour, Madame Frenchie. J'm'appelle Evangelique.*

Comment vous appelez vous?

Avez vous une chambre ici pour forty *dolleurs per nuit pour une* lost soldier?

Pas de cockroaches *s'il vous plait!*

(now to the audience) 'Cause I grew up with roaches, dude. Roach shit on the counters every damn morning. Seen roach shit on my toast before! I didn't eat it. Heard roaches poppin every time I went to cook a pizza in the damn oven.

Oh. Speakin of pizza. *(She dials.)*

Hey there hamsom. Well I think you're hamsom. You goin to pick up lunch today? Well damn, it's your turn soldier. Yes it is. You are teasin me, because I'm PRENINT.

Yes he is, he is kickin like a cancan dancer today. Yeh, mebbe he's gonna be gay thas okay, every girl wants a gay son to go shoppin with aha course I'm kiddin I would drown him in the river if he was that, without a second thought YAH, well listen are you goin to KFC? Or Jimmy's? Okay. Well get me the chicken burger thing, grilled.

No, I don't. I give ya the money when you bring me the food, loser.

(She sings.) Kentucky Fried Chicken finger lickin good...
(She looks at the computer longingly, makes sounds of an inner struggle.) Ohhhhh...

Don't do it don't do it do *not* google yourself, girl…

> *She googles herself, mouthing the spelling of her name as she does. Goes to first site.*

Whew! Six hundred thousand on me on Google here. Six hundred thousand.

I guess that'd make me famous. WORLD famous.

> *She reads.*

"Are you looking forward to the release of the photos of that soldier getting screwed? By Froggle."

"She's the hamster-faced twit in the Iraqi prisoner photos. There are pictures of her getting nailed, and it looks like they are going to be released."

> *She reads.*

"Drown the slut in acid, she should be hogtied, damn she's ugly I'd put my wang in her ass she is the ugliest female I have ever seen drown that bitch in acid I'd rather cut her head off and fuck her neck hole, show her a fucking donkey, she's inbred poor white trash from West Virginia! Did she get beated with an ugly stick? That soldier's my kind of girl stupid and willing to please—we need more like her and fewer like Hilary and Laura kappa kappa kunts! She's a trailer whore; even a dog wouldn't hump her! She needs her hole beat oh so hard, I think she's HOT! Stupid egocentric pitiful excuse for a human being and worst of all a feminist! I want to fuck her, kill her by fucking her continuously, cut her buttocks into four parts fuck each part fuck to the mouth tear out her vagina."

Whoa. I guess if I was an actor I would call that a bad review. A real bad review.

> *Long beat.*

You must all be liberals, what wrote them comments on me. PEACE PINHEADS.

Pink cotton candy cowards afraid of bein at war.

Afraid of your own SHADOW.

Tell me how much you care about them Iraqi men when they are sawin the head off a one of our boys. Tell me fuckin that.

If all of you was right here in front of me now what I would say to you is one *thing above all:* I am NOT ugly. I am at least a six and a half out of ten I was voted a six and a half outta ten at my school, it was just a real skanky picture. I could shoot that damn photographer! You just take out your driver's license or your passport and tell me if *you* don't look ugly. I *hate* ugly women, women who don't take care of themselves I am not that woman. I have always took care of myself. And strong? I am like piano wire. I could see if I was *fat* y'all hatin me so much, but I don't have an *ounce* of fat on me.

So what gives? What gives, dudes? I am not an ugly girl and I am definitely *not* nor have I *ever* been a feminist. I hate feminists, man, now *feminists* are UGLY.

Thas why they don't like men, they can't get theyselves a man. Is that why you think I am a feminist because I am a soldier? I am a soldier because I love my country.

Because I grew up singin "God Bless America" every single day of my life.

And pledgin allegiance to the flag…

…every ever lovin day of my twenty-three years and so when I seen the call, when the recruiters come to town so handsome and real nice talking to me so nice like Tom Hanks style I said "sure, I'll do whatever it takes to protect my country." I wasn't doin nothing anyways, just working at the Dairy Queen. "Hello how are you today? We got Peanut Buster Parfait, Strawberry Sundees, Brownie Explosion." Hell, I wasn't doin nothing for my country working at the Dairy Queen except makin it fat. And there was no way in hell I was going back to work at that chicken factory. So I signed up that day. *(She sings/chants:)* "I used to be the high school queen. Now I got my M16." That there is a jodie; a kind of motivational chant we sing in the army. Or: "Walkin tall and looking good, ought to march in Hollywood. Lift your head and hold it high, 3rd platoon is march-ing by. Close your eyes and hang your head we are marching by the dead." That one is sad, you know, respectful. And then? There is: "Flyin low and feeling mean. Find a family by the stream. Pick 'em off and hear 'em scream, Napalm sticks to kids." Shhh. We ain't sup-posed to say that one no more but we do, 'cause, well it's tradition, just part of being in the Army. And hey, we don't really mean that, most of us love kids, if kids gets hurt, we feel real bad.

> *Pause, does busy work.*

If things don't go well for me in court, I am up shit creek. Me and my boo, up the shitty crik.

I am *no* feminista.

And… I… am… not ugly.

Man I tole my sister when she went on Larry King to tell him that that is a bad picture that I do *not* look like that and she forgot!! My blood just boils thinking that that homely picture is how everyone thinks I look. And that makes Charley look bad, right? That he got it on with a *dog*. Thas why he has cut me off. I've written him fifty-two letters since he went to military prison, but he don't answer them. I tole him in the letter, I will wait for you the whole eight years, you takin the heat for Condoleeza me and the baby, 'cause the love we found in Abu G. is like Romeo and Juliet.

And we was makin our little G.I. I *hate the* media for makin you ashamed. Ashamed of being with an ugly girl. That burns me more than any other part. Your daddy is a war hero. He gonna get a purple heart eventually, that's what someone who I will not name in very high up position tole me that we would eventually get citations for service to military intelligence and even medals because we are takin the fall. I am willing oh yes I will take the fall for my country any ole day. I am like Joan of ARC being burned at the stake. With them pictures and the whole world wide web hatin me and havin to be a secretary I took the fall but I am not goin to prison I'm going to QUEBEC. Yah, I gotta plan to excape to Canada, I'mona lie under a truckload of Hostess cupcakes or field tomatoes and I'm goin into exile like Napoleon; and like Napoleon, I will return one day, an American hero.

I seen an angel.

I had a lot of hash in me but I seen an angel with eagle wings flying, soaring through Abu Ghraib on that night. And that vision assured me that vanquishing the enemy, vanquishing evil was what I was born to do.

None of them higher ups have spoke to me since it all came crashin down on my head. Since they moved me here to push around paper; I been waitin on their call, but the only person ever calls me is Mommy. And my lawyer. He says I am a scapegoat. And he won't let me up on the stand because I won't act like I'm retarded, which is what he wants me to do, so I won't be held accountable; I'll tell the truth. And that is not what anyone wants to hear.

Wonder if I'll be sentenced to jail for eight years like Charley. It's funny, you know, if things had gone different for me, insteada working in an office and waitin for my trial I mighta had a TV movie made about me, too. She is truly a hero she is, and hey, did you know she's from West Virginia too? Yeah. I reckon Jessica Lynch is America's sweetheart. I am America's secret that got shouted out to the world. And they is not happy about that, not at all.

And that is why they gonna make an example of me.

But one day, I'mona be in the history books. *You wait and see.*

I'mona be a war hero; like Annie Oakley.

I was in that in high school, *Annie Get your Gun,* I was one of the chorus singing; our lead was real good, Lisa? She tried for "American Idol": "Anything you can do I can do better, I can do anything better 'n you." Or what's that one from *Oklahoma?* "I'm just a girl who caint say no, I'm in a terrible twist."

I am going to be *remembered.* But first, we gotta find a way to somehow, make them pictures disappear. 'Cause: The thing about them… pictures.

I look at her, me, that homely little private with the thumbs up.

And the naked Iraqi men,

And…. Well it's like a dream they are telling me I had?

But I don't remember it like that?

And they are sayin: "no this is the dream you had"!

Because they can doctor pictures you know. They can do anything they please.

And those forces that do not want

Girls in the army—wanted the world to see them pictures.

Okay, okay, I'mona be honest with you… in the fact of it,

That is what I did, for one second they said "give us the thumbs up, baby."

So that's what I did. For one second of a whole year, dudes. And *that* is what everyone sees? How would you like your weirdest second, like, played out over and over all over the world… for all of time, dude?

Like those dreams about yourself where ya did something WEIRD something you would never do? And ya wake up and ya feel uneasy and you are glad that nobody was lookin in your dream? And ya just wanna forget it and ya do, because dreams, they just disappear, don't they?

>   *Long beat.*

I'll tell you what most people don't know. It got a hell of a lot worse than that.

That is for pussies. So what they were naked? So? They get naked every time they have a shower. So? And as far as me laughin and pointing at the guy's willie? Well tie me down if that's the worst thing that happened to 'em in Abu G. they be lovin it.

But that is not the style of girl I am, okay? I respect men and their privates and I do not nor have I ever laughed at a man's willie. But these are not men, they are terrorists.

And they had intelligence. They knew who was gonna blow up who and as far as I am concerned I was doin what had to be done, *to get to the intelligence* and that is, according to their culture, me laughin at their willies was worse than a beatin *way* worse. I was softening them up; like you might put out hard butter on the windowsill. *I was doin' what I was trained to do!* I had a smile on my face but this was SERIOUS—INTELLIGENCE—WORK.

And I am very proud to say that the naked human pyramids WAS ALL MY IDEA.

Actually, it's the first thing that come to my mind when I walked into that prison and seen all them men that look exactly alike. I know what might be fun: HUMAN PYRAMID WITH NIKKID CAPTIVE MEN. Because I always did have an interest in choreography, you know? I see people dance, I wanna go in an mould 'em.

And they might not have liked it, but they have learned something useful. If they teach gym, in a school. Or supervise a cheerleading squad.

We was not entertaining ourselves. We was breaking down the terrorists.

And it worked. We did attain information.

And the other...

Takin the guy around on a leash?

Well he called me a dog.

Yes he did. Just like all you losers on the net. Like all those assholes back in Fort Ashby. He knew a little English and he called me a dog so for once in my life I could fuckin give it to him *you think I'm a dog? You think I'm a fucking dog you monkey? Let's go for a fuckin walk you wanna go for a walk?* And Charley and them is laughing and well, I never got laughs before I am not a funny person, and WOW man, getting laughs is the *best high* the guys was laughing dudes, they loved it, so they go: "Put him on the leash." And I do like a sketch, like "Saturday Night Live," like "Oh my God it's time to take the dog for a walk... hey Mom? Did you take the dog for a walk? *Henry? Henry.* Did you walk the dog nobody walked the damn dog I'm walkin' it. Here dog, ya dirty dog. No treat for you today you been a *bad dog*." And I'm pullin him... I was surprised how different is a human neck from a dog neck. With dogs you can pull and pull and they just keep on going not with humans. They necks is soft.

And... well.... It is a weird feeling—made my breathing go—a little funny. Shallow. My voice kinda got full of breath. And I felt like that—Alice in Wonderland from the Disney movie? Where everything was not real and I could walk out anytime and what was behind there would stay there.

I had that over someone else once and that was—Lee Ann Wibby; she was missin' a leg? And she wanted friends so bad and she smelled and she was weird and ugly? Now *she* was ugly, so nobody liked her. So we was bored so we axed her to come to the clubhouse and she come with her backpack and her nightie she thought it was a sleepover birthday and we made her strip and bark like a dog and even lick Ryan's dickie, and there was a moment that I realized she would do anything we said. Anything at all. We burned her clothes? And we took her fake leg off, and chopped it up—okay, I know it sounds terrible but we didn't chop up her flesh leg or nothing—and then we tole her to start crawlin home.

Beat, where she struggles with guilt.

Once in church, we hadda think upon our sins? And I seen her there, she was in the church, and she turn around and she looks at me. And I knew then, that what all happened at the clubhouse had been more than a joke for her. Well sir, I love God with all my heart and Jesus is my Lord so I did pray for forgiveness about Lee Ann Wibby—but dudes, Lee Ann Wibby is an American, she was very VERY different from the APES AT ABU GHRAIB. They was monsters in the *shape* of human beings. They was prisoners of WAR.

So, there I was, little me, in ABU GHRAIB me who'd been workin in the Dairy Queen in Fort Ashby, who had been fired several times from the Dairy Queen, for messin up the Brownie Explosion and I was the BIG boss of these BIG DEAL TERRORISTS, guys who had KILLED AMERICANS. GUYS WHO WERE PLANNING ANOTHER 9/11, dude, AND YOU ARE UPSET THAT I laughed AT THEIR WILLIES?

Beat.

Like I said: We did a hell of a lot worse than what you seen. Or what you heard. What YOU seen is tiddlywinks: we made a man masturbate. Ohhhhh. So SCARY!!! SO? So WHAT? So the frick what? I'll tell you I didn't do nothing to them Iraqis that hadn't been done to me many times at the clubhouse. By my friends, and they still my friends. Yeah. I'm not mad at 'em, it was just a little fun.

Some of the churchier girls'd look down on me for that but hey at least I'm BUSY ON A SATURDAY NIGHT, at least I got a date.

Beat.

See I guess I'm a bit of a martyr. Like them pretty eye Palestinian girls who wear the scarf and walk into a supermarket and blow theyselves up? THAS what I done; I done blew myself up.

I ain't here no more.

See… they didn't like me at first. Charley, and Bruno, and Francis.

Wayne, Ry, all the guys, I walked in? They started with the comments.

Okay, you know what I'm sayin, like I should be cleanin or cookin and what am I doin in the hardest ass prison how I'm gonna wussy out. They didn't like me, they wouldn't talk to me; they stole my food, they hung me upside down, poured water on me in the night. Then they seen what I could do. They seen I was tough. I was as tough and as bad assed as they was. I wudn't afraid of no Saddamite. I may be a little girl from West Virginia but once I was out of the gate and through the lookin glass I just thought of bein in the shack with Lee Ann Wibby and I thought of the Twin Towers and all them people running and I thought I'm takin your soul first. I'm takin your soul down like a big saw can take a hundred-year-old tree down; I'm buzzin you down 'til you ain't got shit left 'til you ain't even human. And then I'mona take you down further.

And then, when we good and ready, we blow your brains out.

And we laugh while we are doin it. Make no mistake.

Because we are rejoicing.

In defeating. The enemy.

Of freedom.

> *Long beat.*

And so Charley and them, they started to think I was okay.

Pattin me on the back, it was like camp.

It was like workin a farm in a way. The animals you gotta just handle.

You gotta do what you gotta do, slaughter the pigs, herd the cattle,

I mean guys like Charley never looked at me back home. Suddenly, a cute guy had a woody for me. I couldn't b'lieve it. I like the way he called me he always said "Private Sexy" like that? With this wicked smile make me melt—so we started doin it up down and sideways, yes, sometimes in front of the RAKEES. Just to fuck 'em up, it made Charley harder when they was watchin and I am NO prude never have been and so he got Ry and Wayne to tape us and at first I was a little shy, but he said "please," he would need it when he was away from me, when he was lonely, he could just pop in the tape and he be fine. so I said, "Okay, for my Romeo," and I let them tape. I just pretended they wasn't there, an I ask you, is there a girl in America that has not been videotaped doin the you know what? It's human nature innit?

> *Silence, reflection.*

They didn't say a word man, everyone ax me wha'd they said when you was trippin on 'em but they didn't say—hardly nothing. It was just this silence. Make me feel weird, that silence, you know? This thought run through me once, with that silence? From the History Channel, when the Nazi's there? Made the Jews run. They always had to run everywhere, and so they would run, without sayin anything, with this *look* on they face that is what the RAKEES had they had that look that is what Lee Ann Wibby had when we was choppin up her leg. Made me feel weird. Made me feel…

One of 'em, who the other ones seem to look up to? I think he was like, a holy man. Ronnie goes to him: "Hey you. Wise man, mullah. Fuck him, fuck your friend there in the butt, man! Do it *now*," and the translator tells him and the guy, he speaks English anyways, right? So he turns around and says, in this soft doctor voice:

"There is no reason for this. This I will not do for your entertainment."

So you know what Ronnie does? He hadda take a shit so he takes it right there in a bucket hands it to the man, the guy who spoke English, and Ronnie makes him… eat his shit! Starts shootin at his feet. "*Eat it, eat it, teacher.*" So he eats… Ronnie's shit and that shit stink, dude. The funniest was Ry; he gets the other Rakee to kiss the holy man with his mouth full of shit? And Manny throws up. Oh my God we razzed Manny about that all night!!

> *She reflects for a moment, and to her surprise, a feeling of remorse wells up inside her. She remembers the man speaking—both DAVID Kelly and NEHRJAS look at her.*

"There is no reason for this. This I will not do for your entertainment." Him sayin that, won't leave my head, you know? I wake up in the night sometimes, hearin him say that. I have to take a Percocet, make that go away.

This paper pushin is so damn *boring!* I am a mover, dude, I likes to move all the time you never see me sittin any time of day, that's what my mom always said "That girl don't sit unless she shits." I think I am messin it up, too.

    Silence.

"JUMP ON THE CAT."

That's what he said my best friend Ray it was on Easter Sunday? I had on my lilac dress and my little white shoes my hair was permed and I ask him how does he like my new lilac dress innit pretty? He goes: "*Jump on the cat.*" Cat's there, breathin too fast, I don't know what Ray done and I'm like "NO, I don't wanna mess my shoes," he's like "JUMP ON THE CAT."

So I takes off my shoes and…

So soft. Like the Rakee's neck. Like Lee Ann Wibby. Same feeling in my stomach. Same feelin in my heart. Same fast breathin… like the Rakees when we was…

"There is no reason for this…"

I am thinking very serious about splittin, don't tell nobody. I'm goin to Canada. To French Canada just gonna blend right in. In Quebec City won't nobody know me, they like Americans there! I say I run away from the Mafia. I'll get a nice French Canadian guy, a Pierre, to take me in. An I could have the baby, and we could bring him up Eskimo.

They take me to prison, they take away the baby.

And they take away my baby. Over my dead body.

And I could work in his corner store. *Depanneur.* I seen it in the Quebec dictionary.

I would like that. Sellin cigarettes. And candy bars. And milk. And bread. And the baby grow up to a little French Canadian, but really an American boy, help out his mom. Same customers every day. "*Bonjour, Madame Claudine! Comment savah?*" Nobody knows me. And every morning, when I get up and start the *café*, I will pledge allegiance to the flag; I will pray to my American God. And I will make American coffee and when I look in the mirror, to wash my face, I will take a minute to go back through the lookin glass. To those secret nights when my breathing went funny and there was dry ice in my heart and I did GOOD for my country. I said NO to the enemy.

I said you don't MESS with the eagle you don't MESS with the eagle, dude or the eagle tear your eyes out and that's what I did I tore 'em out and I flew, man, for just that night I flew through Abu G. my wingspan like a football field.

And I soared through the air.

Long silence.

'Til I crashed back.

Through the lookin glass.

Fade to black.

Harrowdown Hill

Dr. DAVID Kelly, a Welsh/Englishman of fifty-nine,
a microbiologist, sits against a tree. His pant leg is
pushed up, and there is a slash at his wrist, but not
much blood. There is a little blood on his knee. His glasses
are beside him, on one side, and his watch on the other.
There is a bottle of water beside him, and an empty bottle
of pills. He sings the first few lines of "The Ash Grove" by
John Oxenford.

DAVID The ash grove how graceful, how plainly 'tis speaking
The wind through it playing has language for me.
Whenever the light through its branches is breaking,
A host of kind faces is gazing at me.

I've solved the riddle.

Can you believe it?

I have been trying to solve the bloody thing,

since...

Oh! Look at that. *(shows leg)* Quite nasty... I used to scream at the
sight of my own blood, as a child, did you? But somehow as an
adult, it soothes me—lets me know I'm—not made of...
Plasticine—does that sound koo koo?

> *He breathes in.*

Smell the roses on that breeze. Oh they smell so... red, don't they?

You know, this is my first moment of peace since the invasion.

And, in case you're wondering, that's why I am hiding. Hiding in
Harrowdown Hill. Sounds like a children's book. Looks like one
too, doesn't it? All these ash and oak trees, little woodland creatures
running about, wildflowers everywhere mad scientist hiding.

It's the best hiding place in the world, don't you agree? Ohh! Did
you ever play sardines, as a child? I did, it was my favourite hide and
seek game—how you'd start out all by yourself and one by one they

would quietly find you and squish in, and you'd be this big squished group all just breathing, trying not to giggle while the last seeker walked round and round, calling out. I loved that game. I loved… hiding. The idea of being… invisible, you know? There and yet not there? The way I am now.

Oh, they will never find me.

Not behind that thorny thicket.

Not the baddies.

Nor the good…

Until tomorrow morning.

They'll find me about eight o'clock.

And I'll be dead by then.

Dead at first light.

D-E-A-D.

I can't fathom it, can you? I mean, as a scientist, I know it to be true, I know exactly what's going on inside my body, how long it will take for my liver to fail, the loss of blood to have its effect. I know that if I am not found, I will certainly die, and I accept this, fully, but you see… I can't imagine… it. It's the—forever part that stumps me. I mean, it would be one thing if I was dying just for a while, even for five or six years, until this whole mess in Iraq is over, as long as I knew I would be coming back, it would be *fine*, I could cope with that…. The idea of *never ever*… seeing orange juice again, or my daughter's eyes, or wild honeysuckle… the never never neverness of it all, you know?

If someone had told me when I was sixteen, "David Kelly you will die in a forest when you are fifty-nine, after your fifteen minutes of *world fame*"—I wouldn't have believed *either*… the forest or the fame.

Me? The quiet little Welsh boy? How could I ever be of consequence in the world?

Perhaps I'll come back as a great spotted woodpecker, make lots of noise, and fly anywhere I want to. I always did love flying dreams, do you have them? Perhaps it'll be like that.

I'm sure it'll be like that.

Yes.

So it's not so bad for me. It's them.

My wife. My daughters. My sister.

The shock.

The... shock.

The loss, I suppose. The grief.

The tawdry... talk, all the bloody nattering.

"Oh, yes, remember that mousey British scientist Kelly? He killed hisself. Remember? He was the weapons inspector who got himself into all that trouble blabbing to the BBC? Saying there were no weapons of mass destruction in Iraq, calling Tony Blair a stinking liar—they found him, dead, in the forest."

Was it suicide?

Or WAS IT MURDER?

Some will say it was bloody murder, it was MI6, it was the Iraqis it was the Italian Secret Service, the CIA.

They will cite the email I wrote this morning to my friend, Judy. "There are many dark actors playing games." The other emails I wrote this morning show I was fine. I was strong. Very excited to go back to my beloved Iraq. My work is not finished yet. I have no psychiatric history whatsoever. After all I've left no notes. For my family. Whom I love. Whom I... adore.... Why, oh why would I take my own life? Others will say it was certainly suicide. There will be an inquiry, which will declare to the world that yes, of course it was suicide.

That sad little Walter Mitty of a man just couldn't take the pressure. The pills, *(He points them out.)* they will say, are proof positive— two co-proxamol will be found in my stomach; they will point out the slashes on my wrist, the ulnar vein cut, the knife that made the slashes, a knife I was given when I was twelve years old... they will say I was a man defeated: the brutal interrogations, the bloodthirsty press, the threat of being terminated. I was depressed, exhausted and in despair. I was a weak man, a meek man, poor in character, of course I committed suicide.

But almost nobody will believe it. There will be a rock song by a member of the band Radiohead, art installations by angry Germans, television movies and the Internet will roil with talk of the murder of David Kelly by men in black. That's how I'll be remembered. The mousey scientist who set off a storm. Another casualty of the War in Iraq. After all, what is one fifty-nine-year-old slightly potty scientist? Hundreds of British lads have been killed already. Hundreds of thousands of Iraqis. Why should I make a noise? Many men don't make it to my age anyhow; I've had a good go.

When we are young, our death is impossible... we see our end as a calamity, don't we? Like the sinking of the *Titanic*. Part of the... salve of aging, is that our death starts to make a sort of sense. Like one's child going off to university. Yes, it's a bit sad, but not tragic. It's as things should be.

> *Evensong from a church in the village—or bells.*

Is this too much to ask? That you witness my death?

It's a terrible thing to ask, I know.

But... I am asking.

Because.... Well, I don't want to be alone. Is that weak?

I can't have my loved ones here because, of course, they would revive me.

Do you remember Bobby Sands? He and some other IRA fellows they were on a hunger strike for better conditions in prison, and they insisted their wives and mothers and sons and daughters promise them that when they became unconscious, they would not be revived. An almost impossible promise to make, can you imagine? But the family of Bobby Sands, they kept their word. Maggie Thatcher, of course, didn't give way. And Bobby Sands died.

Does his death have meaning? I believe... that it does. After all, he is remembered.

You see, this might be the only way I can have an impact, the only way I can make up for what I did not do.

> *Beat.*

I'm beginning to think that it's the greatest sin of our time.

Knowing, and pretending that we don't know, so that we won't be inconvenienced in any way. Do you understand what I am saying?

I knew. Oh the things I knew.

And I did nothing.

Can you imagine, knowing, knowing that a man is torturing a child in your basement, and just going on with your life? Knowing it is happening right under your feet, as you wait for the kettle to boil, as you tuck your own children in bed, as you work in the garden the dim light is always there, the muffled sound of her screaming, you pretend to yourself "It's the crows on the line," but in your belly you know it is her *agony*, he is cutting off her fingers one by one, pulling out her eyes, her teeth, unimaginable torture and this is something you know for certain, others may guess at it, many deny it, but you know it for certain and you don't tell anyone because you might lose something if you do. Your carefree life, your ability to be happy, your job. Your job. And if you lose your job you lose your pension. And you don't want to lose your pension. They said, they admitted they needed to sex it up, for the people, the people of Britain were not going to send their boys to a war they didn't believe in, they would tie them down rather than see them go, they said we had to fill the people with fear, we had to remind them of World War II, they had to understand that the threat of Saddam was like the threat of the Nazis. We all knew that this was not true. We all knew that the *casus belli* was a lie. What could we do, we had no power, we just shook our heads, and scurried away, little mouse men. We were not to talk; we had taken a vow of secrecy, if we wanted to hold onto our jobs, we had to keep our mouths shut. So. I put my head in the sand.

I told myself "I am for the invasion, Saddam is a monster no doubt about that, regime change is a must. The people will dance in the streets, if only for a day," I told myself: "They are good men, Bush and Blair, and Berlusconi. They want good for the people, they will topple Saddam, give aid to the new government, and be on their way."

I told myself lies.

Have you ever?

Have you ever told yourself an unforgivable lie?

Long beat.

A few weeks before the invasion, a friend of mine, the American ambassador to Sweden asked me what would happen to *me*, if Iraq were invaded and do you know what I answered? I said I would probably be found dead in the woods. They'll make much of that, after my death. It'll be all over the Internet. And the funny thing is, I can't explain it. I was making a kind of morbid joke. But maybe I knew something that I didn't know I knew, you know?

At the start of the war I would wake up at six, watch the news every morning, from my bed, each day's smooth, velvety-voiced account of bombings, and casualties, and "collateral damage," I watched, hoping against hope that things would… would improve, but it soon became very clear to me that things were far, far, far, far worse for the Iraqi people than even I could have imagined.

What did I do?

Did I go scream in the streets?

Did I write to the papers?

No.

I did nothing. Nothing at all.

I became… clumsy. Yes, that was the only giveaway, I burned myself on the stove, I cut myself chopping onions, and I fell flat on my face on the pavement, I crashed into people in hallways, sat on my glasses, dropped the phone constantly, dropped and broke plates, couldn't eat without dribbling, staining all of my shirts with food, I was in great demand. Flying to conferences all over the world. With stained shirts and broken glasses. The truth about Weapons of Mass Destruction that's what everyone wanted to know, I skirted the truth, bobbed and weaved but I loved to hear my own voice. Loved to be regarded as the expert the world expert on biological weapons; I was even nominated for a Nobel Peace prize, for my work in Russia, ten years before: uncovering Stalinist secrets, disarming the next Black Plague and that is how they always introduced me, I talked to the press incessantly, my words always precise, witty, always filtered, always bloody lies. Walked through a screen door in Houston, Texas, and fell into a river in Bern. Bit my tongue constantly. That was maybe the worst.

And then one day, one sunny June morning I was in New York City
just leaving the U.N. I received a phone call, from my dear old friend
Jalal. He owned a bookshop in Baghdad, called Al Nakhla, in
English, the Date Palm Tree it was my favourite bookshop in the
world, and I have been to almost *all* of them, no, I truly have! It's
what I do in my downtime, wherever I am—well Jalal is one of the
most kind and joyful and learned men I have ever known, he had
about five degrees in literature he had thousands of books. And he
had read *all* of them. He had books that were hundreds of years old,
written in blood; he had giant books it would take three men to lift,
tiny books with pages like moth's wings that would fit in the palm of
your hand, they smelled of history, books in every language, illustra-
tions that would make you weep, each room had a theme, the art of
Babylon, American cowboys, Chinese fantasy, Antarctic cuisine,
everything you can imagine, it was a kind of magical labyrinth, and
the delicious cooking smells, of kubbeh and mint filling the shop—
I would browse for hours, in a kind of trance and then, Jalal would
insist I stay to dinner, with his family, oh, you would love his family—Marwa, well Marwa, and she wouldn't mind me saying this at
all, is sort of an Arabic Lucille Ball—she would turn the act of getting ice out of the fridge into this huge comic routine, have us all on
the floor shouting with laughter—and she was an amazing cook, and
their daughter, Sahar. I think she had just turned thirteen last time
I saw them, she was obsessed with *Anne of Green Gables* her life's
dream was to dye her hair carrot red and to visit Prince Edward
Island, in Canada, we hatched a plan, to bring the whole family on
a ship to the Island and rent a farmhouse together for a summer, we
were really going to do it, and Tabarek—the naughtiest five-year-old
boy in the universe had to climb everything he saw—tables, fridges,
walls, people, I became... so... so close to this family, bringing gifts
for them all, never the right gifts of course, I'm terrible at gifts, being
treated to little plays and songs, I loved that family, they became, in
a way, my best friends in the world. He said they were watching her.
Sahar, his 13-year-old, she was a very pretty girl, like a magazine
model, I suppose, tall for her age, beautiful smile, a woman's figure
but still very much a little girl, a happy child who loved her stuffed
animals, and he said the American soldiers were watching her.
He said they looked at her like a wolf looks at a rabbit. They were
ravenous. There was evil in their eyes, he said, Blood. He said he
planned to move her the next day, to take her to another town,
to stay with her cousins. He wanted to know if I could speak to

someone. I said I was sorry, but there really wasn't anyone I could speak to, even if they had been British. And then I reassured him. I told him not to worry; I said they were probably bored young hicks from Alabama who couldn't put two words together. Intimidating young girls—their only entertainment. I reassured him that they were carefully monitored by their commanding officers, and they would never dare approach her. "If you could only see their eyes," he said. Even when he was with her, they would look her up and down, and say what were clearly crude things and laugh. She would go home and cry in her mother's arms. I told him again not to worry. I was sure everything would be fine. Not two days later, according to the *New York Times,* four American soldiers confronted Jalal and his daughter Sahar outside his bookshop. Took them inside. Said they were looking for weapons. For insurgents. "There are only books, please take all the books you want," said Jalal. Once in the shop, two of them took Sahar aside. The other two rounded up Marwa and Tabarek, took them with Jalal into the basement. And shot them. The killer climbed the stairs and said, "I've killed them. They're all dead." And then the four soldiers threw Sahar to the floor, raped the child. Put a bayonet through the child and shot her in the face.

They then set fire to the bookshop.

He is having trouble breathing.

The press initially said it was the work of insurgents.

"The terrorists." Until two other soldiers from the same battalion as the killers were captured, and beheaded on camera. One of the four killers, tormented with guilt over his comrades deaths, certain it had been revenge for the murders, confessed. Well. The day I heard what happened to my beloved friends was the day I blew myself up. Was the day I met Andrew Gilligan of the BBC and I told him the truth.

To *hell* with vows of secrecy, professional confidentiality.

To *hell* with my pension.

To *hell* with my life as I know it.

The *truth* the truth must out.

He yells.

I want to tell the TRUUUUUUUUUUUTH.

The truth the truth the truth the truth the awful horrible terrible.

Truth truth truth truth truth truth truth.

And out it poured.

Whatever he asked me? I told him the truth.

Yes I had seen the dossier before the invasion.

Yes I had had serious concerns.

And *yes* they ignored them.

And *yes* they *lied* to the *people*.

And *yes* tell the *world*.

And you know how it went, he told the world, he shouted it out but I was his secret, his secret source. And just when he was about to be sent to prison for not revealing his source I did the right thing, I wrote the letter.

The letter to the ministry explaining that I was the source.

I was the source and I was not ashamed. *I am not ashamed.* I naively believed they would protect me: they threw me to the hounds. I was ready. I sat before Parliament on the hottest day in ten years, I was lashed, I was blasted, I had crashed through the looking glass; I was confused and exhausted, and I could barely be heard. I could not raise my voice. They even turned off the air conditioning so that I could be heard. Everyone was wilting. "Will you speak up please?" I was not capable. I was a tired old man and I wanted to go home. They very nearly defeated me. But do you really think, do you really think I am so pathetically poor in character that I would *kill myself* because the parliamentarians BULLIED me? When I had so much left to do? When I have a family I worship? Listen: Do you say that a soldier who loses his life in the name of freedom, truth and compassion, has *killed* himself?

When I finally *talked, told the truth,* I knew that I was risking my life. And I knew, absolutely, that it was worth it. I accept what has happened, do you understand?

I accept what has happened. I sat in my chair this morning and I *made a choice*. I made a choice to stop—fighting; to allow whatever was to happen to happen. Because I realized that they would never ever leave me alone. What I had done, in their minds, was treason. I would be like what's his name, that character in Greek mythology that is tied to a rock in the ocean and is doomed to have his liver pulled out by ferocious vultures every day for eternity—they would never ever leave me in peace. The only way to defeat them is to disappear, do you understand? To be present, but invisible. Like hide and seek. I'm here. But you can't touch me. I see you, but you don't see me. I am the ghost of Harrowdown Hill.

I hope it's a searcher who finds me. Please let it not be my daughter. She does know my walking routes. We have walked this route together, many a Sunday afternoon, although never this far. Never through thickets. Is that her calling me? Or is that my imagination? Please God let it not be my daughter.

What time is it? Four forty-two in the morning now. The police are everywhere, and I can feel the fear in my family. I hear their worried voices. I am so… deeply sorry that it has to be this way. I hope, I know that they will understand. And one day they will see clearly that although I look as though I've lost, I have won. I have solved the riddle.

A song: there is a song that I need to sing, a song that I used to sing when I walked with my daughter. Searching for buttercups:

A… dahh dahh dumm. Yes, yes, that's the melody. La laaa… yes.

Breathing is quite difficult now. My organs are failing.

Less oxygen in my blood, heart tired out.

Thank you. Thank you for witnessing… it won't be long now.

Within a few hours, my flesh and blood body will cease.

But I, David Kelly, I am *here*, and I promise, I will always be here.

He weakly sings:

The ash grove how graceful, how plainly 'tis speaking
The wind through it playing has language for me.
Whenever the light through its branches is breaking,
A host of kind faces is gazing at me.

He falls asleep, into a coma.

Blackout.

Instruments of Yearning

A beautiful, but haunted Iraqi woman of about fifty sits in a chair by a window overlooking a huge date palm tree. She is a woman who has a strong buoyant spirit but she has suffered immeasurably. There is a small golden pot of tea and a glass saucer and a tiny glass with a gold rim. She drinks tea as she talks. She smiles at the audience:

NEHRJAS   One of my earliest memories is drawing in my own blood.

Drawing a flower, a daffodil for the school nurse. Looking back, I can't imagine why they were taking the blood of a child at school. It wasn't enough to send to a lab, just enough to draw a daffodil. I drew a daffodil because that is my name:

Nehrjas. "Daffodil" in Arabic.

My Western friends tell me that there is no such name in English, although there are many of flower names.

There is Rose.

There is Dahlia.

There is Lily.

There is Violet.

There is Viola.

I laughed when my British friend said to me "Now what is the correct spelling of your name, dear." How can you talk of correct spelling when you transcribe Arabic into English? It is phonetics only.

What is fascinating to me is that women are names of flowers, but not all flowers; because if you are English and you are named Daffodil people will laugh. That is what my friends have told me. And if they want to insult a man, say to a man that he is not masculine, they call him "pansy" but not rose. Or tulip. And another thing I have observed is that a woman is never called after

a tree. Only a flower. Because the purpose of a flower is to attract
a bee.

And the tree,

The tree stands alone.

Blissfully—alone.

The tree provides air.

And shelter.

And food.

So I think, all mothers should be given a second name after
a tree.

Do you see the tree outside my window? Ah, isn't that a beautiful
view? I can see the whole world from here.

This tree, this is a date palm or the Nakhla. So tall, elegant, proud
and beautiful, and how should I say it—enduring much like
a woman. A fully-grown tree, like a fully-grown woman does not
need much of anything, save a little rain now and then. Like me:
Some people feel sorry, "She is old, she is over fifty now, can't attract
a man," are you joking with me? You think I want to attract a man?
Oh yes I am dying to wash his feet and make his bed and cook and
clean and soothe him and praise him and say he is so strong and
sexy and smart and bury myself alive! Although I loved—adored—
my husband, he was an extraordinary man... I will tell you about
this later... it was only once I was all alone that I could live in the
land of myself. People ask me "Aren't you lonely, with your husband
dead and your children elsewhere? Surely you will die of loneliness."
I am not lonely; I am a full-grown tree.

Just as the leaves breathe out into the air and fill it with healing
substances I breathe out my memories, good and bad. It is not
company I want. It is to bring back what I can never bring back.
And anyway: You will know that I deserve to be alone. For I have
committed the greatest sin of all.

She takes a drink of water, or does a chore.

So, the date palm tree. When she has age, she doesn't need much.
But, when she is young, she requires a great deal of special attention
to truly flourish and bear fruit. Like every young girl, like my

daughters, oh so much attention or else they wilt like flowers in the heat and have such anger and screaming at their mother. Every year, an—arbourist, is that the word? Good for me, ah? Has to climb up each tree at least four times. I watch them from this window. It is one of my greatest joys. The lowest row of drying leaves must be removed of course, sometimes I lean out and I would say "You missed one, right there!" and then in April this tree has to be— pollinated. In August, the dangling dates have to be positioned—so they are supported. Otherwise they just—you know—hang down and be ruined.

In September or October, the dates are harvested. Such a happy time. It is an amusing puzzle to me that in the West dates are only eaten by the average person in something you call "date squares." They say they are too sweet and rich for the Western palate and yet what about this "fudge"? When I was in America they sold this fudge everywhere. Is this not over-sweet and over-rich and over-creamy with zero nutritional value?

I don't get it.

English is a funny language. How is it permissible to say the idiom "I don't get it," but if you were to say, "I don't catch it," the whole room laughs.

So. Back to blood. One of the exhibits at the Umm Al-Maarik Mosque in central Baghdad was a copy of the Koran written in Saddam Hussein's own blood. This is ironic. This is blasphemic. Why do not the heavens rain tears and the earth vomit blood at this outrage? The Holy Book written in the blood of the Devil?

I wonder who told him to do that? Or did he think of it himself?

Did a mullah demand of him to do this, as a proof of his love of Allah?

Or did his mother or his wife say to him you must appease the mullahs or they will defeat you. Because they *will* defeat you. If they want to defeat you.

They are as water, which eventually defeats everything.

>   *Silence.*

Is there anything more powerful than the love of God?

I want to tell you a secret. Before I had babies I did not really believe in God.

I said that I did. Everyone thought me very religious. I went to the mosque. I prayed five times a day. I observed all the rituals: the food, the dress, all of it.

But in my heart? In my secret thoughts? I did not believe. I thought to myself I thought maybe this is mass delusion. As Karl Marx has said, "the opiate of the people." And then I hated myself for even thinking that: "Who do you think you are," and I would smack myself in the face. I wanted to believe. I prayed to Allah to help me believe in him. I prayed so hard I drew blood from my lip. But He would give me no help. And I felt like an imposter.

Pretending. I would never tell my secret to anyone. Even my husband.

Because an infidel has no friends.

My soul was an empty space. Until

I had my first child... a son,

I looked at him and I saw Allah.

I cannot explain this—it is beyond words.

My faith came back like a great river, which has been dry and begins again to flow. And every time I felt it drying up, because of the terrible the unspeakable things that were happening to my people. I looked at the face of my son, and my faith returned. Listen, no matter how bad things get in your country—I know you have your terrible sex and blood crimes—there are many gang shootings and your prisons are full, but you cannot I do not want to be rude but I am telling you that you cannot even begin to imagine what life was like under Saddam Hussein. To even say his name it makes my stomach sick. And I will not offend any of God's creatures by calling him a beast. There is only one word for such an evil human being. *Shaytaan.* Satan. Because Satan means to me the human embodiment of evil.

And I do not mean by this ignorance.

I remember the day of the coup. I was in a taxicab; he was taking me to school. I was a high school teacher then, when I was a young mother. The radio was on but I was not listening. Suddenly the cab driver stopped. He got out of the car.

He cried, "All of Iraq is burning," the Baathists, with the support of the CIA, had killed the president and all the ministers.

We were entering the age of darkness.

I laughed out loud when Saddam's statue was toppled. And I cheered when the Devil was turned into the rodent he truly was and captured in the claws of the Eagle. I was overjoyed to see elections: hopeful. I would like to have voted. I thought maybe, maybe there is at last some light. But this moment of light and ·hope was an illusion, how stupid was I, ah? To think for even one moment that life might be better? That the Americans and their murderous brothers the British cared about us, about our freedom, our children? This hope was a flash, a lightning flash in the pitch dark, and it is gone.

Iraq is once again hell.

Could hell be as bad?

Those who supposedly came to liberate us… it reminds me of a young woman I know who had been taken off the street one day by officials and raped many many times. At the end of the day they threw her out of the car to the side of the road, in the countryside. She crawled along, bruised and bleeding, half naked, and soon, a car stopped. A very kind and gentle man with his family stopped and helped her to the car. The wife covered her and they took her to their home nearby and the wife drew a bath for her and said they would call her family while she cleaned herself and rested. As the children played in the house, the man sneaked into the bathroom and raped her again in the bath. She did not cry out because she did not want to embarrass his family. And when her own family arrived, thanking this man so profusely, bringing him gifts—

Those who say they have come to save us have come to destroy us.

So. My sin. *Hal Haram.* The worst sin of all.

On the day of the Devil—the Baathist Coup, they rounded up anybody they believed was a threat. That day, my husband went into hiding. I myself was arrested at work, taken from the school, interrogated and after a few days released. My mother thank god was

with the children. Oh yes! Everyone we knew was put in prison for
a time; anybody who was thinking, intellectual, active. Anyone who
was political and could be a threat. Anybody who was a member of
the Communist Party.

Everyone I knew was a member of the Communist Party. Wait. I can
see you are pulling away from me when I say "Communist." But this
is not the Communist Party of Stalin, or Mao or Pol Pot, or post-war
Europe, far far from it.

All of the kind and thinking and peace loving people in Iraq at that
time were members of the Communist Party. You would all have
been members of the Communist Party. Oh yes. Ask anyone now.
The Communist Party was the only one that welcomed people of all
religions and backgrounds. And it was the only party prepared to
fight to the death to free the people.

It broke our hearts that the United States land of the free, home
of the brave—liberty and justice for all was supporting the coup.
After the coup, the CIA gave the secret police a list of the names of
everyone in the Communist Party; they were making the Baath
army, and their torturers all-powerful we had to be very secretive.
We had to let our babies cry at night so that their cries would cover
the sound of typing. If the secret police heard typing, they would
arrest us immediately. One day they took my little brother. He was
a silly boy, he liked to dance with girls and drink alcohol and wear
expensive clothing and he was at the university. He was taken.
We did not know where he was. We received a phone call in the
morning. "We are sending him home in a taxi." We waited all day.
The taxi arrived. The taxi driver said *Allah akh bar*. "There is a
God"—because my brother was, incredibly, still alive.

We rushed him into the house because if the neighbours saw they
would shun us—they would be afraid of guilt by association. And
he—he was so badly beaten we couldn't recognize his face, and he,
he could see nothing. My other brother cried and my mother said,
"Don't cry! This is the way men learn to be men." It seems harsh, but
you have to understand the way we lived, and what it was to be
a man.

So, the monsters we lived in fear of were the Baath secret police,
"Jihaz Haneen." If you can believe it, in English? The Instruments
of Yearning. Can you explain that to me please? The torture jail was

a fairytale castle, from long ago where the king had lived—we had not liked him either, he was Saudi but he was nothing compared to Saddam. The gardens were tended by a master gardener, a true genius of nature. And so the castle was called The Palace of Flowers. Until the Dark Age. When it became The Palace of the End.

"Qasr al-Nihayah." Iraq's own house of horrors; our children weren't afraid of fictional witches or monsters, those stories are only for peaceful places, our children had nightmares about the Palace of the End. "O people of Iraq…. By God, I shall strip you like bark, I shall truss you like a bundle of twigs, I shall beat you like stray camels…. By God, what I promise, I fulfill; what I purpose, accomplish; what I measure, I cut off."

So said al-Hadjadj, the newly arrived governor of Iraq, in the year 694.

So said Saddam.

So said George Bush and Tony Blair.

And here we are. So.

As I said, my husband had been in hiding ever since the coup, as he, at that time was the great, visionary leader of the Communist Party. Oh yes! He was a beautiful and courageous man. He had a huge popular support, and he was poised to begin a revolution. Yes, it would have taken years, but it would have happened, and so many lives would have been saved. We all believed fervently in this revolution. Watching our friends and loved ones disappear or at best be tortured beyond recognition, it gave us hope. So we would do anything to protect this possibility.

You must understand that countless lives depended upon our success.

Hah. I just thought of an amusing story. A friend of mine who lives in America now, he was in Washington D.C. at a party or event and the wife of U.S. Ambassador to Iraq in the sixties and seventies said of the Baathist coup: "It was a terrible time, my God we lost all our electricity. We had to go around by candlelight and it was freezing at night." My friend just laughed and laughed. He said: "Madam, for you it was electricity. For us it was death."

So imagine me, a young and very beautiful woman. Well it's true. You see me now, in my fifties, I am a handsome woman. But then? *Kullish Helwa!* I have pictures. I had now four children. My son, fifteen, Nahdne. I had a two years old girl, Laila, and a precious eight years old son, Fahdil, the light of my life, my helper, my inspiration, my mischievous monkey. Also, I was eight months pregnant.

Well. One day, as I knew they would, they came for us. Thank God they let my mother take Laila, but they took Nahdne from school, and me from my home.

I had been boiling an egg. To have with a date. It's true. And in came the thugs.

And you know who they were? You might wonder, who were these secret police? How did they collect so many eager criminals and sadists? Well I tell you they were the local bullies. One of them I recognized, he used to bother me when my brother and I went to the movies. He would harass me, say filthy things, and my brother gave him a warning. That's who it was, the losers, the ones who would torture animals, those people you avoid. So. They took us to the prison.

I remember thinking thank God they do not have Fahdil—he will know when he comes back to an empty house he will know to go to the neighbours. He had been carrying some mail from one house to another. Young boys would always do that for us they were so fast and so small. So we are driving up to the castle.

Like an American horror movie. Now, the castle has three stories. The highest floor is where they would take you to talk. The surroundings were quite nice. A reasonable conversation. If you were willing to talk, then you talked you betrayed everyone you knew, and you were free to go. Sadly, some were so afraid of torture that they talked immediately. I don't judge anyone. Everyone is different, and torture changes everything. Then, if you didn't wish to talk, they would send you down to main floor. It was what we call Torture Lite.

Beatings. Broken bones. Nails removed. That kind of thing. And if you still didn't talk, you were sent to the basement. There were bodies everywhere. Bodies of people you knew. Once you have smelled the smell of death, of mass murder and suffering, nothing smells sweet again, not ever again. The memory—not the memory, the actual smell… remains always, somewhere in every breath you take. So. At first we were sent to the highest floor. And we refused to speak. So after an hour or so we were sent to the first floor. A small room. Me, my fifteen-year-old son. And my torturers. The first thing they did. They held my belly in their hands. They laughed. And they said "Who did this to you?" I turned to my son. I said, "Do not listen to them. They are half men." And then I said, "It is the child of my husband." And they asked to me "Where is your husband?" I said that I did not know. They started only by jumping on my feet. And hitting my son's nose with a hammer. They hit him until he could not feel it. So he stopped crying out. And then they stopped hitting him, because they knew it did not hurt anymore.

We were… inside hell now. I only prayed I would not lose the baby. My son and I looked at each other. I knew he would be strong. This went on for hours.

Needless to say I was raped many times in front of my son. They forced him to watch. But he did not see. His eyes looked into my eyes only. So wise for fifteen.

And then, when I thought they will let us go. At this point they did not want to be seen killing women, especially pregnant women, or children. They were trying to win the hearts and minds of the people still. And this is what is taboo in every culture in the world I think. The last taboo. And just at that moment when the head torturer said to me, "We will let you go, but next time…" in through the door comes another with my eight years old son Fahdil. They had caught him as he was running with the mail. Someone must have pointed him out to them. Someone had betrayed us. They had blindfolded him. He was very frightened of the dark. They had beaten him about the face even before bringing him in. My son. They let me embrace him once. First: they asked him to tell them where was his father. He said he didn't know. He had been well trained. Then they began to beat me again. And rape me again. To scare him into speaking. To protect his mother. But he knew. I turned my face to him to make sure he was alive and you know what he did? He smiled at me. He kept smiling to give me courage. And he was eight years old.

> *Fi 'aalamen azlamat marayaahu*
> *Ayyu nashidehn lam yanbajas 'aassalan*
> *Wa anta tafar fi sanayaahu*
> *In a world whose mirrors are dimmed*

What song did not flow with honey
If you were to smile your praise upon it?
      —Nazik al-Mala'ika: a great Iraq poetess

So. They began to torture my son Fahdil. They said all we want to know is where is your father. You tell us you can have bread and water. About six hours later. He said he would tell them. I was almost relieved. But then he told them a lie. They gave him bread and water while the others went to find my husband.

He whispered to my older son that the reason he told the lie was although he knew they would keep beating him, he thought that the bread and water would give him the strength to keep the secret to endure more torture. And so they came back. And so beat him more. I was tied up, on my back, forced to watch, as was my older son. Well Fahdil lied three times. Three times he got bread and water. But the third time, they were onto his trick. They were furious. Now they beat him hard, with the full strength of men. He said to my older son, "I'm dying" he said, "I feel death around me. I want you to take care of my mother and little sister." They thought what more can we do? What can we do to break down this child and his mother?

Meanwhiles, they had taken away my older son, Nahdne, I did not know where. What they did then? Do you notice I have no fan here in my apartment? And it is forty degrees outside and probably forty-five in here?

There was a fan in the torture room. Right above me where I was tied.

They grabbed little Fahdil by his shirt. He was able to look at me one last time, my precious boy, he looked into my eyes with his beautiful sorrowful eyes and he smiled. I said, "I love you my son." He did not scream, he did not even whimper. My son was more brave than many full-grown men, and he was eight years old. They turn him upside down, and then they tie him to the ceiling fan—upside down. They tie him to the ceiling fan and they turn it too fast. So my son. Is spinning. He is spinning round and round. I cannot put into words the feelings inside me.

I was praying and he was praying. We were in the hands of the devil no doubt but we had faith that we would be delivered—faith was all we had. And neither of us will speak. If we give in, we are giving not

only our lives but the lives of millions. It would be like giving up
Nelson Mandela, you understand? It would be like saying yes; you
can go and murder these million children. To save ourselves. And
I knew, I was quite certain they would not kill us because it was so
deeply in my culture to never harm a pregnant woman or a child.
I thought we will survive this. My son will be known forever as the
most heroic child ever lived. He will become a great leader. But he
kept spinning.

My son who loved to write stories and draw pictures of animals.
Who named our black and white cat "Jawhar": "Precious"... loved
geckos, gave every one he saw a name, and you know in Iraq they are
everywhere, but he had a story for each one, and always hoped to see
a cheetah, for there are a few cheetahs in Iraq he would pray to Allah
to see
a cheetah and have a running contest for he was a very fast runner...
spinning upside down over my face. And still, I did not speak. The
baby was turning and turning inside my belly. I fainted many many
times that day. After hours and hours of the spinning. My son, of
course, was unconscious. And they threw him on the roof. It was
cold then. It was winter. He had no coat, of course. And they carried
me up to an attic room, just underneath the roof, and tied me down.
And still I did not speak. For days and days I lay there, the only thing
keeping me breathing, was that I could hear my son coughing on the
roof. That gave me such happiness, to hear him cough. I knew he
was sick. He probably had even pneumonia, but the coughing meant
that he was alive! And as long as he was alive when they let us go
I could nurse him to good health again. I was sure they would try
to look like good-hearted men, and at the very last minute they
would let us go. I was so sure. And that is why. I did not speak.
Every hour was like a day, every day like a year, his cough was
stronger and louder and then it began to get weaker.

And weaker.

Why did I not speak then?

And weaker still.

And then he did not cough anymore.

> *Long beat.*

They came in, laughing.

"We found your husband anyway you foolish woman. And oh… we are sorry about your son, we were going to let him go today, but he must have had a weak constitution. He is with Allah."

The Palace of the End.

A long silence.

Sucour? Is that the word? For sustenance of the soul? Oh! Alliteration. Like Shakespeare. I like that in English. Not the same in Arabic. Impossible to explain. So. My succour these days is poetries. I am not talented to write it. But I am talented to learn! I have learned much Iraqi poetry by great Iraqi women. I have memorized by heart. I say it out loud. Every day. To my date tree. To the dead who are all with me. To my father, to my mother. To my husband.

And always, of course, to my son.

Long silence.

You might be wondering after that, "Does she still believe in Allah? If she found Allah in the face of her son where is He now? Where are her rivers of faith?"

Isn't my date tree so beautiful? There are more than 300 varieties of dates. Can you imagine? When I was pregnant with my oldest son I wanted to try every kind of date. But I stopped at one hundred. Yes. *One hundred.* Actually, they all taste pretty much the same but don't tell an Iraqi I said that!!

You know that for hundreds, thousand of years, the dates, together with camel milk was the diet of the Bedouins, just as potatoes was the diet of the Irish.

To harm this tree, it is unforgivable. A military saying from ancient times:

Do not kill a woman, a child or an old man. Do not cut a tree.

What happened to that? That is only a joke now. That is "collateral damage."

One of the sights that made my blood freeze during the long Iraq-Iran war in the 1980s was the orchards of date palms with all trees—with their tops taken off. Bare.

Now the U.S. army has torn down thousands of trees on the road leading to the airport. For security they say. But a palm tree is not like your maple tree or your evergreen it cannot hide anybody.

Sound of a bomb.

Of course my faith was gone. The riverbeds were dry. But my soul was not empty and I will tell you why. Many nights I had a dream, that when I would finally die, which happened in the first Gulf War when I was killed, right here, by an American bomb, I would finally again see my son. I knew that he would smile to me just as he did on my darkest day, a smile that said: Forgive. Forgive yourself Mama, because I forgave you. And he takes my hand and together we fly. We fly around Baghdad putting the crowns back on all the date palm trees.

It is very nice, this flying. Just the same as in your dreams. Only better. So we flew. For a while. But after a while he said "Mama, you must go back to Baghdad—and watch over our people, with all the other ghosts. Me, I am a child, so I can go to paradise now. But you, you must watch, because the worst, Mama, the worst is yet to come…. You must watch until there is finally peace. But I will wait for you." And so I am here, watching. With the thousands of other ghosts who are watching with me. There are more every day. Do you see them all? They are everywhere, all around us. And when there is finally peace, Fahdil will come again and we will fly together, we will fly through the crowns of the Nakhla and into the eyes of Allah.

More music, and the three performers stand, somehow communicate with each other, and walk off.

The end.

photo by David Laurence

Judith Thompson is the author of *The Crackwalker,*
White Biting Dog, I Am Yours, Lion in the Streets, Sled,
Perfect Pie, Habitat, Capture Me, Enoch Arden in the
Hope Shelter and *Palace of the End.* She has written two
feature films *Lost and Delirious* and *Perfect Pie* as well
as television movies and radio drama. Her work has
enjoyed great success internationally. She is the recipi-
ent of the 2007 Walter Carsen Prize for Excellence in
the Performing Arts. In 2008, Judith was presented with
the Susan Smith Blackburn Prize for the best play in
the English language written by a woman for *Palace of*
the End. She is a professor of drama at the University of
Guelph, and currently lives with her husband and five
children in Toronto.